CAROL VORDERMAN
Maths Made Easy

10
Minutes
A Day
Maths

GW00505931

Ages
3-5

DK

Author Deborah Lock
Consultant Sean McArdle

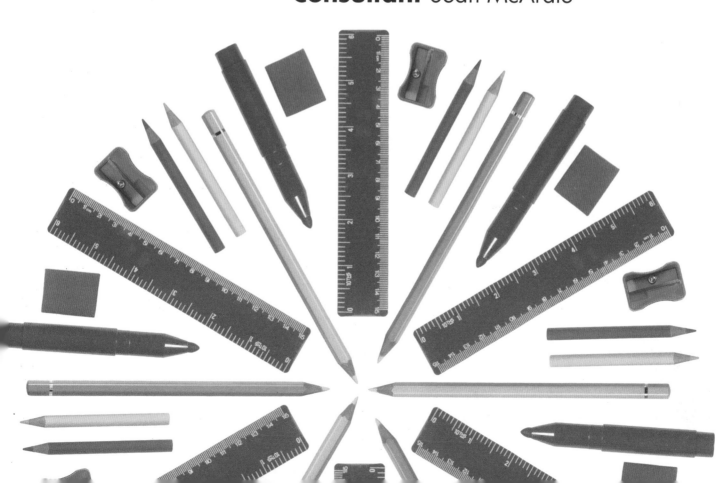

This timer counts up to 10 minutes.
When it reaches 10:00 it will beep.

How to use the timer:

Switch the timer ON.
Press the triangle ▶ to START the timer.
Press the square ■ to STOP or PAUSE the timer.
Press the square ■ to RESET the timer to 00:00.
Press any button to WAKE UP the timer.

 Penguin
Random
House

DK UK
Senior Editor Deborah Lock
Art Director Martin Wilson
Associate Publisher Nigel Duffield
Publishing Director Sophie Mitchell
Pre-production Francesca Wardell
Jacket Designer Martin Wilson
Maths Consultant Sean McArdle

DK Delhi
Editorial Soma B. Chowdhury, Rupa Rao
Design Priyabrata Roy Chowdhury, Anuj
Sharma, Aanchal Singal, Priyanka Singh
DTP Anita Yadav

First published in Great Britain in 2013
by Dorling Kindersley Limited
80 Strand, London WC2R 0RL

Copyright © 2013 Dorling Kindersley Limited
A Penguin Random House Company
4 6 8 10 9 7 5 3
008-186098-10/12

A CIP catalogue record for this book
is available from the British Library.
ISBN: 978-1-40936-781-9

Printed and bound in China
Timer designed and made in Hong Kong

All images © Dorling Kindersley.
For further information see: www.dkimages.com
Discover more at
www.dk.com

Contents

Time taken

Time filler:
In these boxes are some extra challenges. Try them if you have some time left before the 10-minute beep. Or take 10 minutes to do these activities.

Animal families

Baby animals have special names such as cub and chick. How many do you know?

Draw the lines from the babies to their parents.

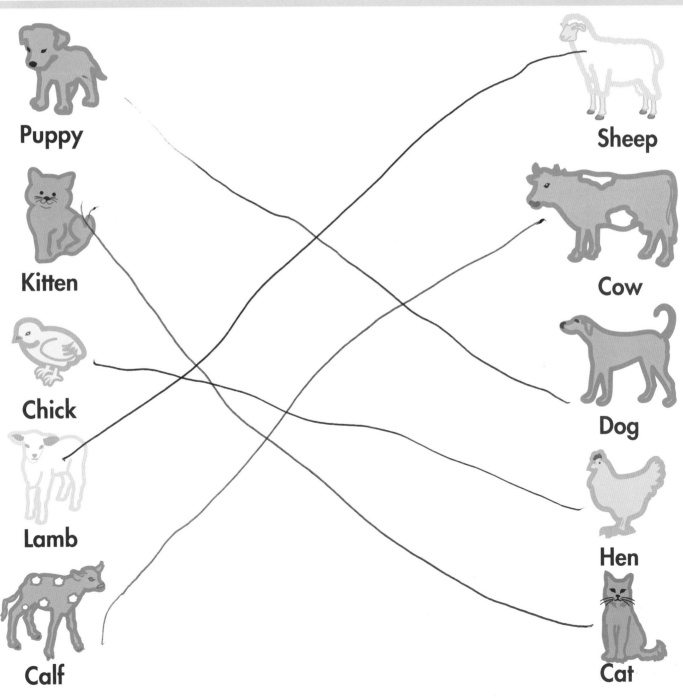

Puppy

Kitten

Chick

Lamb

Calf

Sheep

Cow

Dog

Hen

Cat

Time filler:
Which is your favourite animal?
Ask an adult to help you find out
what its babies are called.

1, 2, 3, 4, 5.
Count how many
babies there are.

1 fawn

3 cubs

2 cubs

4 ducklings

Flower patterns

Flowers are very pretty to look at. They can be found in all shapes and colours.

Connect the dots from 1 to 10.

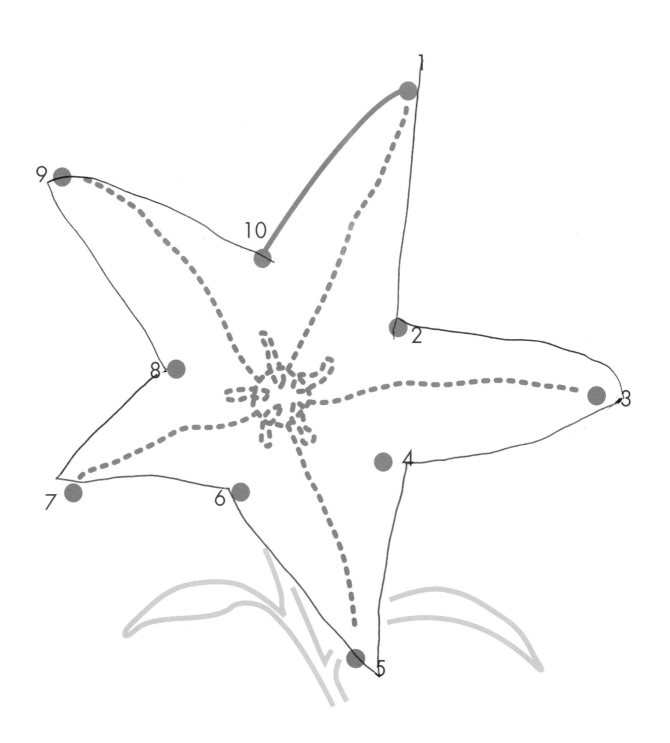

Time filler:
Go for a walk to look at flowers. What colours are they? How many petals do they have? Do they smell?

Read the labels. Colour the flowers using the right colour.

A red flower

A blue flower

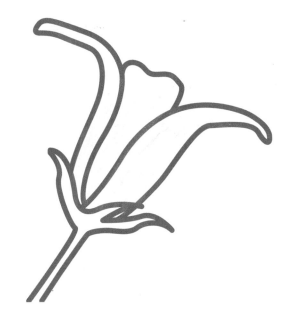

A yellow flower

A pink flower

Fun and games

What do you like to do with your friends? On this page are some of the things you may use.

What comes next?
Continue the pattern.

Draw and colour the same picture.

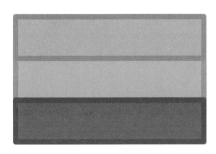

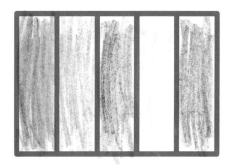

Getting dressed

What clothes are you wearing today? We have different clothes for when it is hot or cold.

In each row, circle the odd one out.

Time filler:
Look inside your wardrobe.
What colour are your clothes?
Do any have zips or buttons?

Draw lines to match
the shoes.

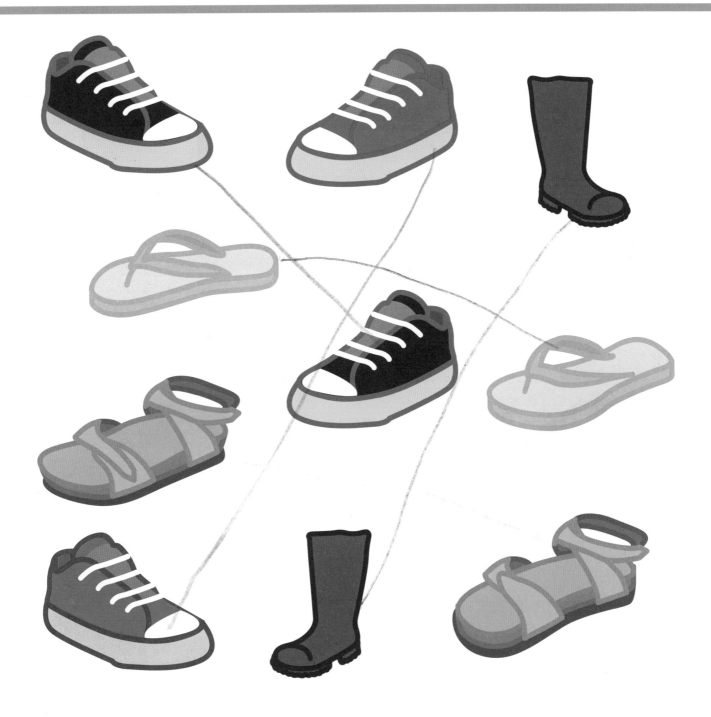

Feeding time

Most animals either eat plants or other animals.

Draw a line from the animal to its food.

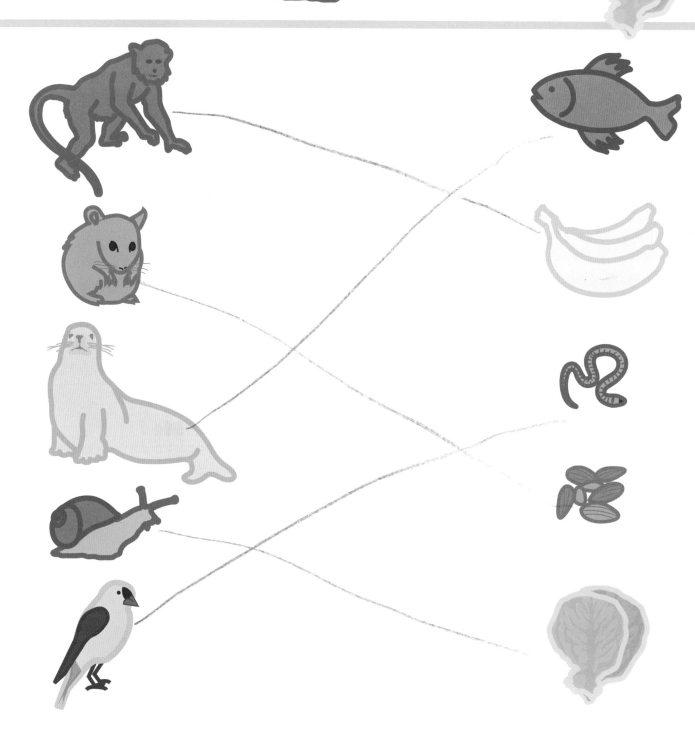

Time filler:
Put out some bread or nuts for the birds. Find out the names of the birds that come to eat.

The zoo-keeper has some fish for the penguins. Show the path he takes to get to them.

Plant shapes

Look to find the plants that are different or the same.

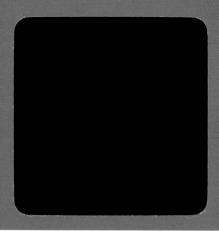

Circle the odd one out.

Time filler:
How many different leaves can you find outside in 10 minutes? Put on your outdoor shoes and then start the timer.

Match the leaves that are the same shape.

At the shops

Do you help put the
things to buy in
the shopping basket?

**Tick (✔) the pictures that
show something is inside.**

Time filler:
Help an adult write a shopping list. Draw pictures of what they need to buy.

Circle three things you would buy for a party.

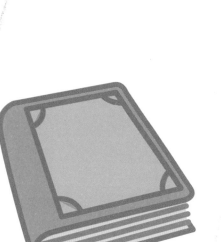

In the bedroom

What is the best thing
in your bedroom?

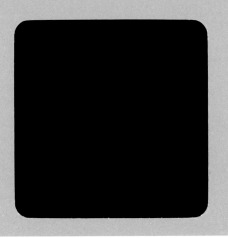

Finish the picture.

Draw a teddy bear on the bed.

Draw some open curtains.

Draw a book on top of the bookcase.

Draw a picture above the bed.

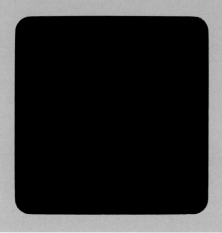

Time filler:
Can you find something in your bedroom beginning with each letter of the alphabet? Start the timer when you are ready. a b c d e f g h i j k l m n o p q r s t u v w x y z.

Let us tidy up! Draw a line to link where the things should be put away.

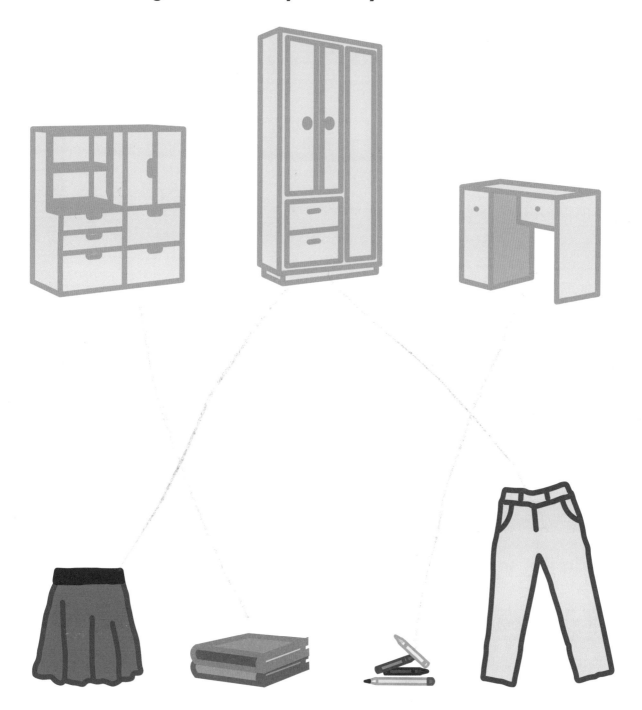

All about me

Hello! These pages are all about you.

Draw you and your family.

Fill in the sentences. Ask an adult to help you.

My name is Etienne

I am 6 years old.

My birthday is on aoog oost 11

Time filler:
With an adult, look at some photos of you and your family. Start a poster titled "All About Me". Stick down some copies of these photographs.

Draw your home.

How many people live in your house? 5

What shape are the windows? Tick (✔) the answer.

Circle ☐   Rectangle ✓   Square ☐

Animal homes

Animals have safe, warm homes just like us.

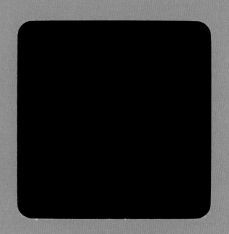

Lead the animals to their homes. Follow the lines with a pencil.

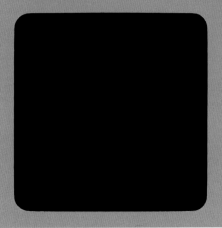

Time filler:
What is your favourite animal?
Ask an adult to help you find
out what its home is called.

**Count the animals
in their homes.**

birds

bear

rabbits

pigs

Tree tops

Trees can grow into all different shapes and sizes. How many do you know?

Circle the tallest.

Circle the widest.

Circle the smallest.

Time filler:
Go outside and try some bark rubbing on different tree trunks. You will need some pieces of paper and some wax crayons.

Draw the right number of apples on each tree.

This tree has 3 apples.

This tree has 5 apples.

This tree has 2 apples.

This tree has 8 apples.

Jobs people do

People do all sorts of jobs. They have special tools to use.

Draw a line from the tool to the person.

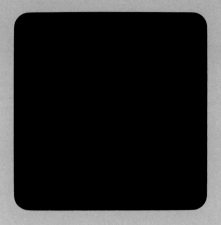

Time filler:
What job would you like to do when you are grown up? Find out what things you would use.

Join the dots from 1 to 10.

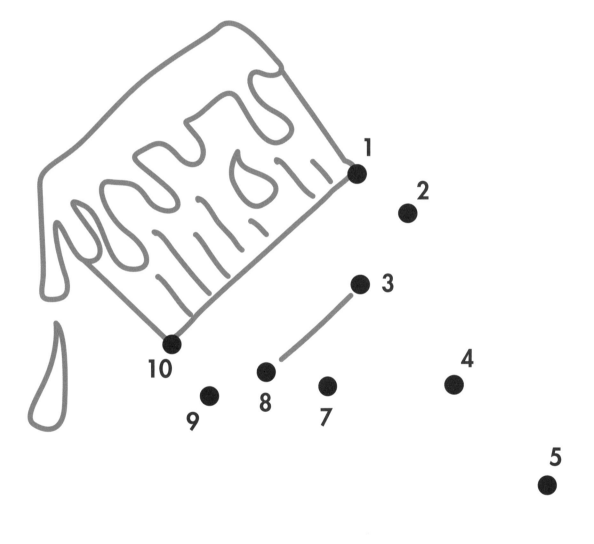

In the kitchen

The kitchen is where food is kept and cooked. What happens in your kitchen?

Draw lines to put away the shopping in the right place.

BEANS

JAM

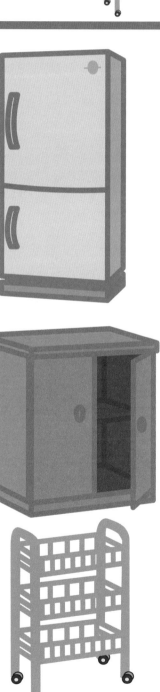

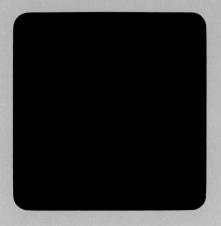

Time filler:
Ask an adult to help you draw a plan of your kitchen. Where is the table? Where is the fridge and the sink?

Match the objects that are the same.

Animal moves

Animals move in many different ways. Some are quick and others are slow.

Continue the lines to show how the animal moves.

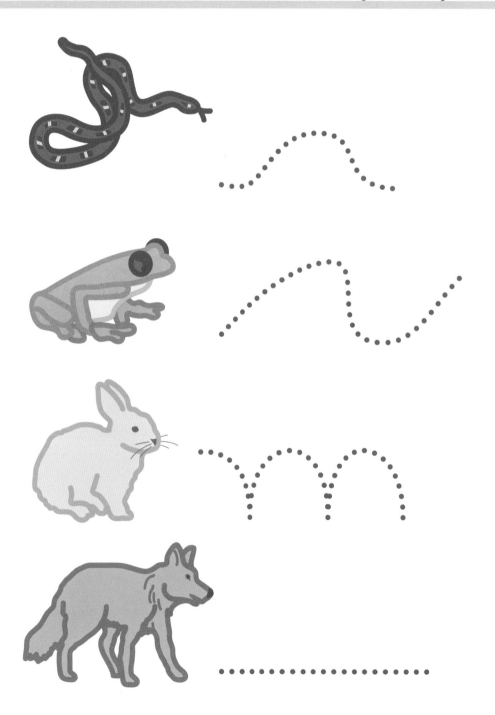

Time filler:
Can you move like an animal? Can you slither like a snake, hop like a rabbit, or leap like a frog? Which animal move do you like best?

Draw the legs onto each body to match.

Pick and mix

Fruits and vegetables are different colours, shapes, and sizes.

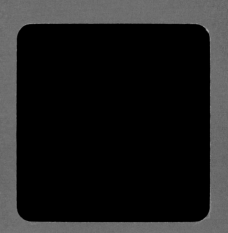

What comes next?
Continue the pattern.

. . . .

. . . .

. . . .

. . . .

. . . .

Pick the fruits and vegetables.
Cross (x) them out.

Cross out 2 cabbages. How many are left? cabbages

Cross out 3 pears.
How many are left?

 pears

Cross out 5 tomatoes.
How many are left?

tomatoes

Cross out 4 oranges.
How many are left?

 oranges

On the move

There are many ways to travel. Which way do you like best?

Colour the vehicles.

Car = red

Bicycle = green

Lorry = blue

Bus = yellow

Time filler:
Go for a walk. Which vehicles
do you see the most?

The lorry is making
a delivery to the shop.
Show the way to get there.

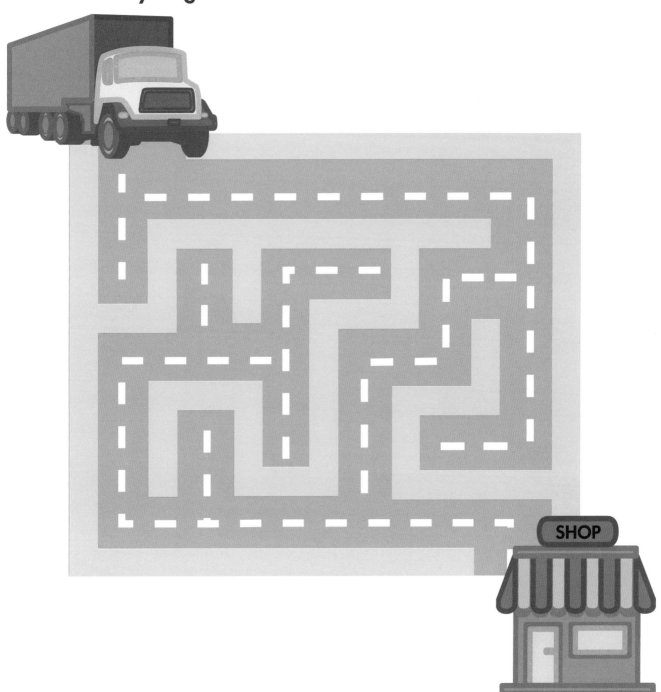

SHOP

Meal times

What is your favourite meal?

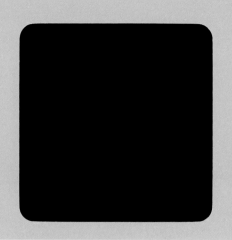

Circle the things you would have for breakfast.

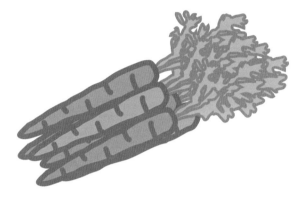

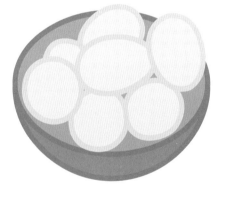

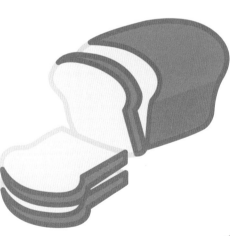

Time filler:
Help an adult lay the table for a meal. Where do the knife, spoon, and fork go?

Pick the food and drinks. Cross (x) them out.

Cross out 2 bottles of juice.
How many are left?

bottles of juice

Cross out 3 bananas.
How many are left?

bananas

Cross out 4 cartons of milk.
How many are left?

cartons of milk

Cross out 5 ice creams.
How many are left?

ice cream

Animal patterns

Animals have colourful coats.
Some have patterns such as
spots, stripes, and patches.

Circle the odd one out.

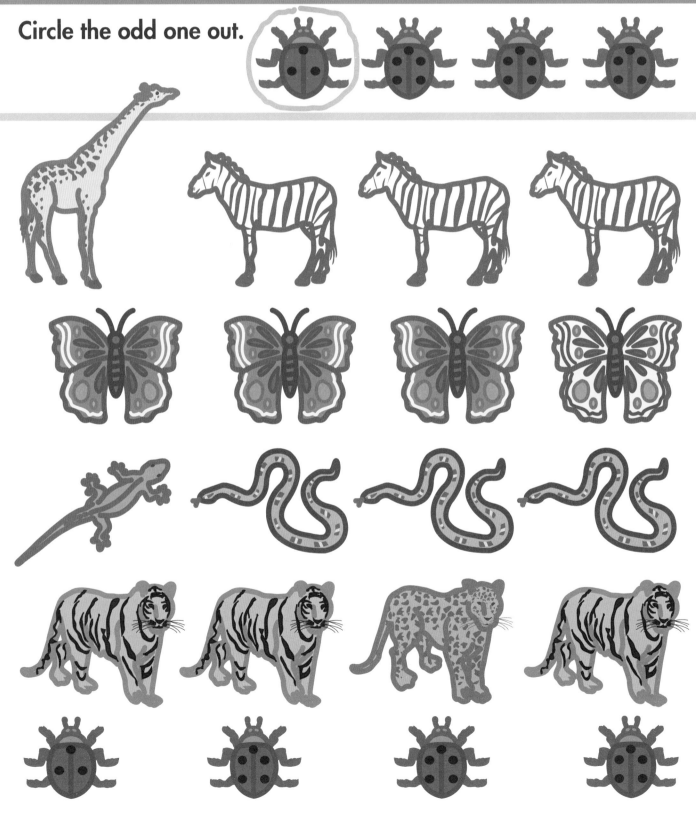

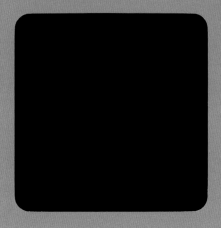

Time filler:
Look at some pictures of animals. What are the colours and patterns on their coats?

Draw the other half of this butterfly to match.

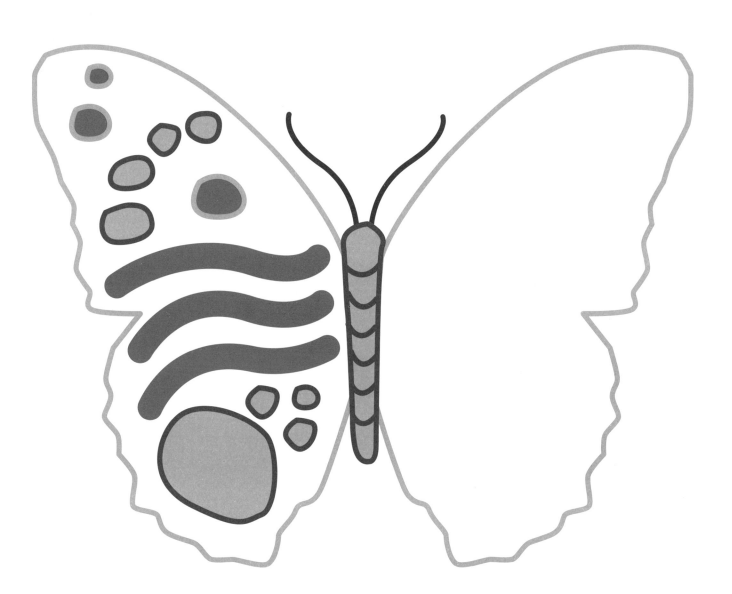

Seed shapes

Many plants grow from seeds. Seeds are all different shapes and sizes.

Draw lines to match the seeds.

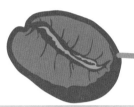 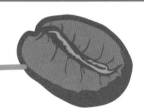

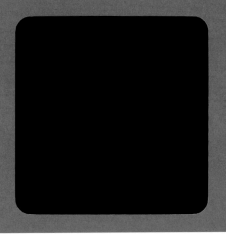

Time filler:
Cut open some fruit and look at the seeds. Place them in order of size from the smallest to the largest.

Circle the smallest seeds.

Circle the youngest plant.

Circle the most seeds.

In the park

What do you do in the park?

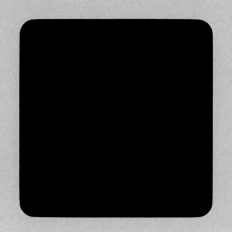

Connect the dots from 1 to 10.

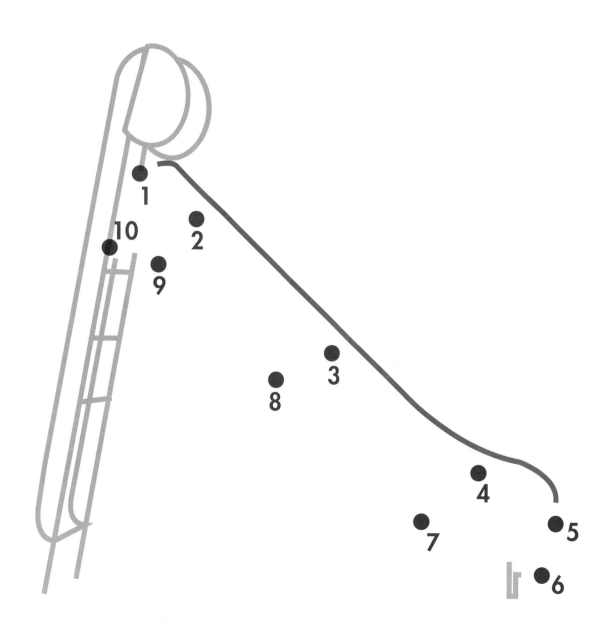

Time filler:
Go to a park. Try to have
a go at everything in 10
minutes. Ask an adult to
tell you when the time is up.

Colour the picture.

1 = red ■   2 = green ■   3 = yellow ■   4 = blue ■

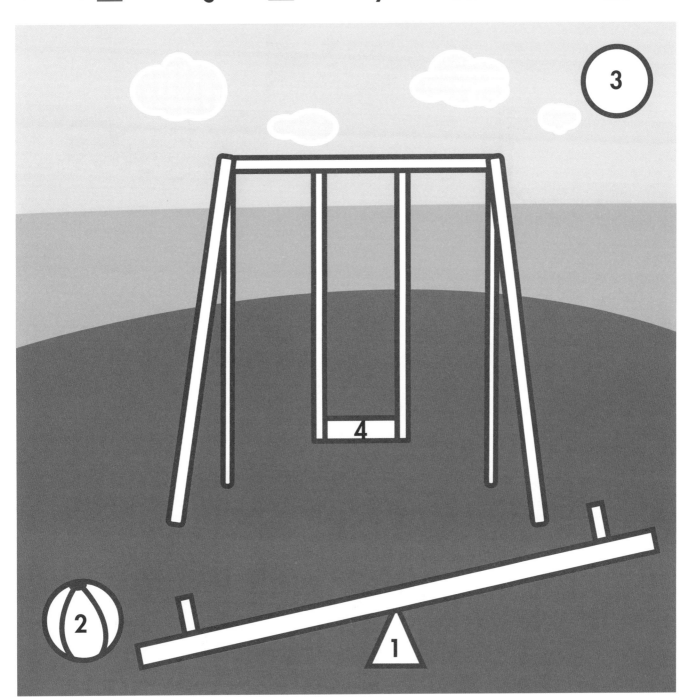

Toys and games

What is your favourite toy?
How long have you had it?

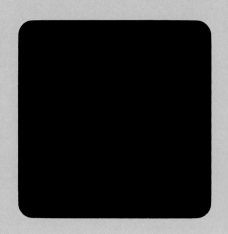

Some of these toys have wheels and others do not. Draw lines to put the toys in the correct set.

No wheels

Has wheels

No wheels

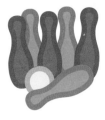

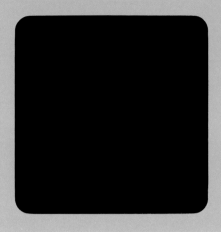

Time filler:
Choose a card or board game.
Play the game with an adult for
at least 10 minutes.

Draw the same picture.

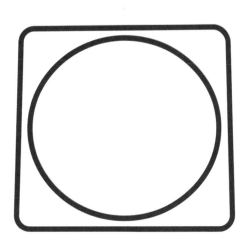

All about me

Look in a mirror. What
do you look like?

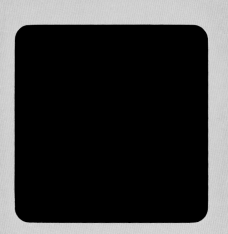

Draw and colour a
picture of your face.

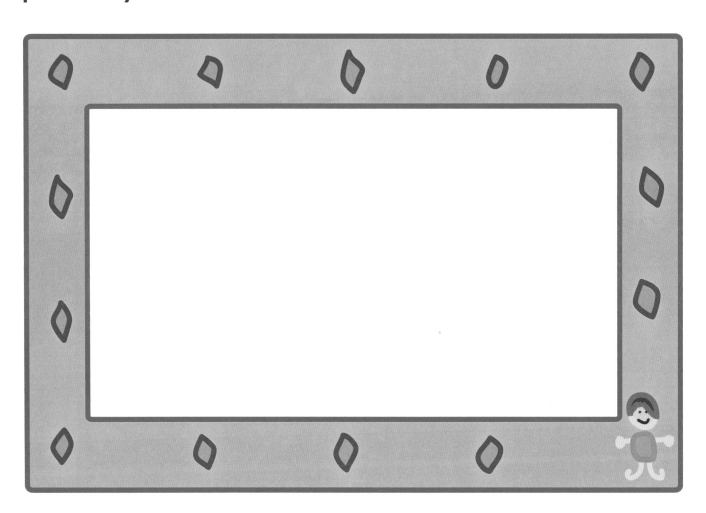

Fill in these sentences. Ask an adult to help you.

The colour of my eyes is . . . .

The colour of my hair is . . . .

My height is . . . .
(Use a measuring tape.)

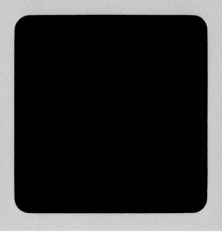

Time filler:
Ask an adult to take some photos of you close up, from a distance, and in different poses. Add the photographs to your poster (see page 21).

Draw a line from the words to the body part.

Ear

Ear

Chest

Leg

Nose

Arm

Hand

Foot

How many ears do you have?

How many toes do you have?

Animal faces

All animal faces
look different. Take
a close look.

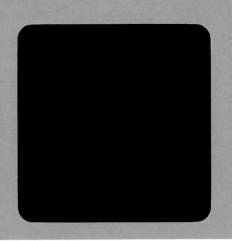

**Draw two wide eyes
on the owl.**

**Draw a long trunk
on the elephant.**

**Draw some large
ears on the rabbit.**

**Draw some sharp
teeth on the crocodile.**

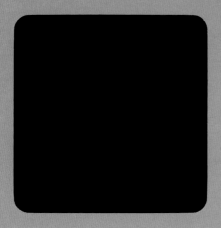

Time filler:
Make an animal mask. Draw an animal face onto a paper plate. Ask an adult to cut out the eyes.

Draw the other half of the lion.

Plant care

Do you like gardening?
Some plants need extra
care to grow.

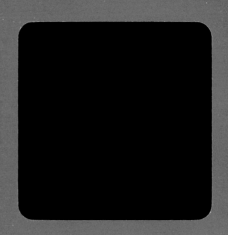

**Circle the odd
one out.**

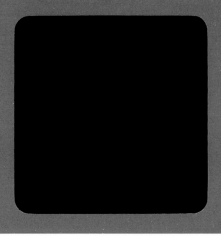

Time filler:
Ask an adult to buy some sunflower seeds. Follow the instructions to plant the seeds in a pot of soil. Put them in a sunny place. Watch them grow. Remember to water them.

Tick (✔) the three things a plant needs to grow.

Sports

How high can you jump?
How fast can you run?
Sports keep us healthy.

**Continue the lines
to show what the
person is doing.**

1.

2.

3.

4.

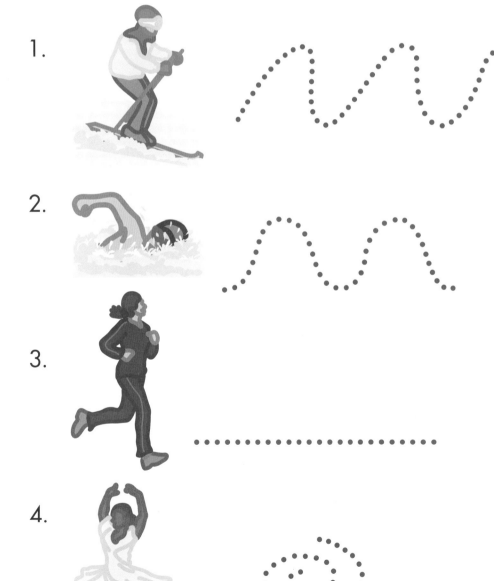

Time filler:
Ask an adult to help you set up an obstacle course. You can jump, run, and hop. Use hoops to climb through and balls to roll. How many times can you go around in 10 minutes?

Who is using this equipment? Draw a line.

At home

How many rooms are in your house?

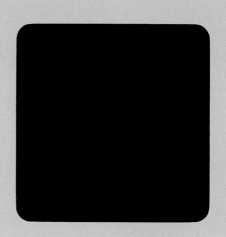

Match the pictures that are the same. Draw a line.

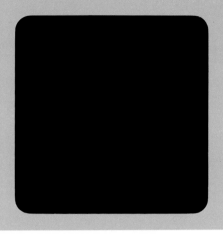

Time filler:
Can you find something in your house beginning with each letter of the alphabet? Start the timer when you are ready. a b c d e f g h i j k l m n o p q r s t u v w x y z.

Count the objects.
Fill in the boxes.

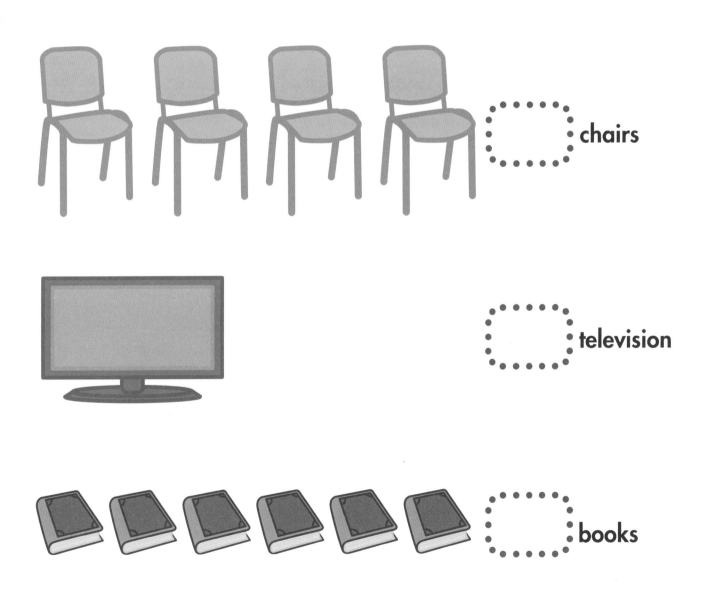

chairs

television

books

crayons

Animal sizes

Did you know that the largest animal ever is the blue whale?

Circle the biggest.

Circle the tallest.

Circle the heaviest.

Time filler:
Draw a picture of a zoo.
What animals would you
like in your zoo?

Put these animals in size order 1st, 2nd, and 3rd. Start with the smallest. Write your answers in the ribbons.

Seasons

The four seasons are spring, summer, autumn, and winter.

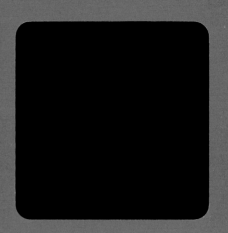

Finish colouring the pictures.

Winter

Colour the branches brown.

Spring

Colour the flowers pink.

Summer

Colour the leaves green.

Autumn

Colour the leaves orange.

Time filler:
What season is it now? Look at the plants. Do they have buds or flowers? What colour are the leaves?

Follow the line from the word to its picture.

Snowy ——————

Snowy

Sunny

Stormy

Rainy

Cloudy

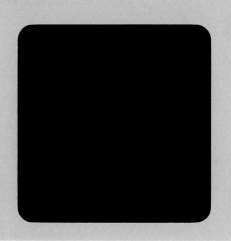

At the beach

Have you been to a sandy beach? What did you do?

Circle the things you would take to the beach.

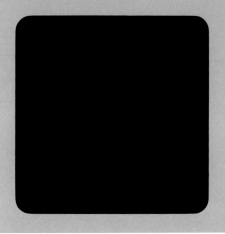

Time filler:
What might you find on a beach?
Can you name 10 things?

Finish the picture.

Draw a ball in front of the beach umbrella.

Draw a bucket behind the spade.

Draw the sun up in the sky.

Draw a towel on the sand.

Draw a flag on top of the sandcastle.

Bedtime

What do you do before going to bed? Do you tidy away toys and brush your teeth?

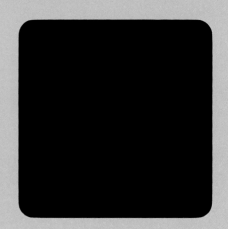

What comes next?
Continue the pattern.

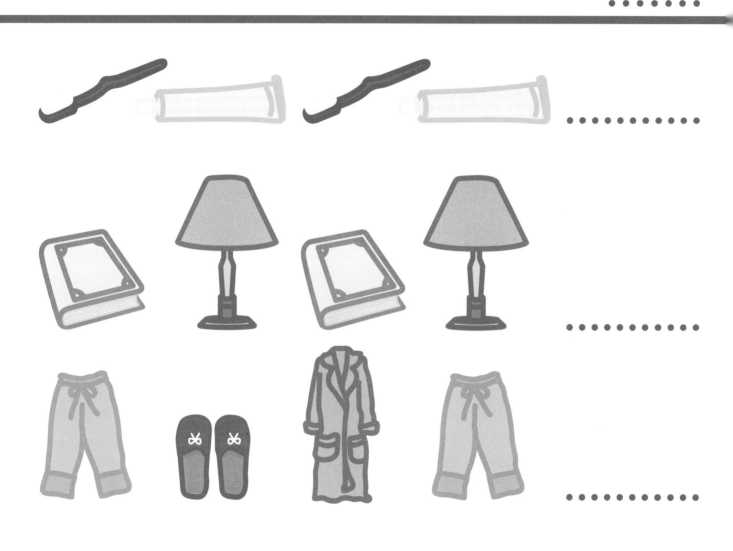

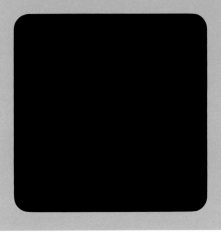

Time filler:
Go outside when it is night with an adult. Is the moon out? What shape is the moon? Point out the stars that are the brightest.

Tell the story.

1.

2.

3.

4.

How many books can you see in these pictures?

What colour are the girl's pyjamas? ....

All about me

What can you do and what do you like doing best?

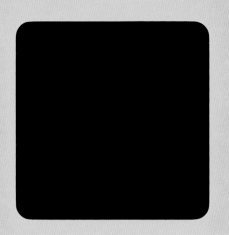

Draw and colour a picture of what you like doing best.

Fill in the sentence. Ask an adult to help.

Best of all, I like •

Have a go at these. Tick (✔) when you have done them.

Can you jump 10 times?

Can you hop five times?

Can you sing two songs?

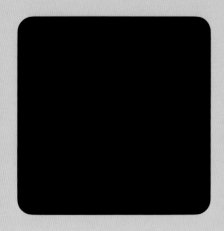

Time filler:
Ask an adult to take some photos of you doing your favourite things. Add the photographs to your poster: All about me.

Draw and colour a picture of you and your friends playing together.

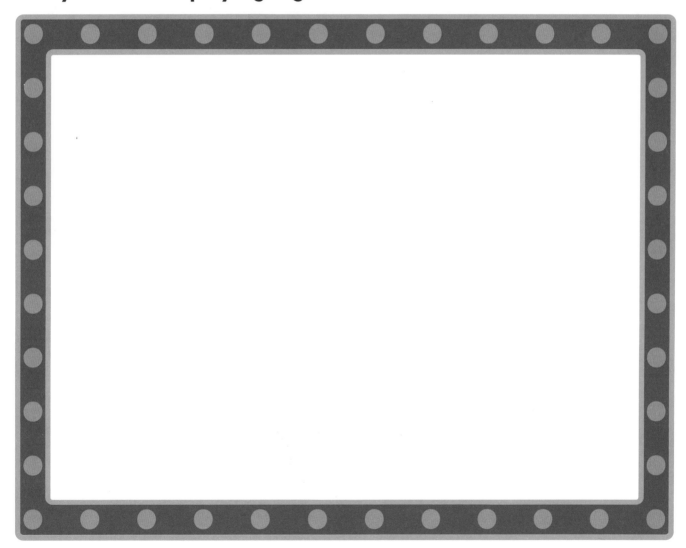

How many friends are there in your picture?

How many are boys?

How many are girls?

66

Answers:

4–5 Animal families
6–7 Flower patterns

4 Draw the lines from the babies to their parents.

5 1, 2, 3, 4, 5. Count how many babies there are.

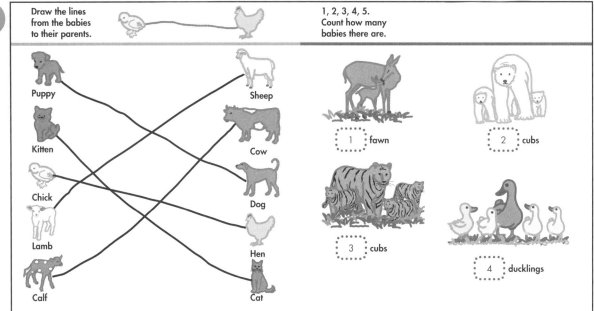

Puppy
Kitten
Chick
Lamb
Calf

Sheep
Cow
Dog
Hen
Cat

1 fawn
2 cubs
3 cubs
4 ducklings

A child learns through fun activities so this book encourages a mixture of practical and hands-on learning experiences. Words are used throughout the book so your child may need help reading.

Discuss the sizes of the babies and animals and see if they can spot any other differences. When counting, encourage your child to put a finger on each animal as they count it.

6 Connect the dots from 1 to 10.

7 Read the labels. Colour the flowers using the right colour.

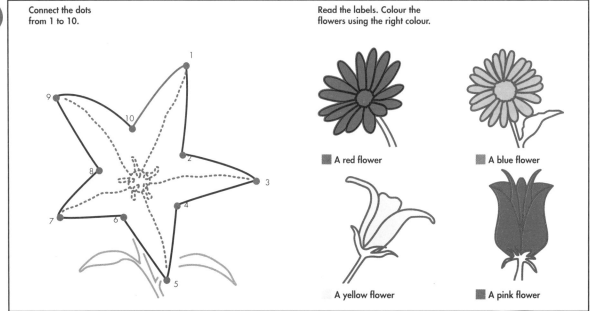

A red flower

A blue flower

A yellow flower

A pink flower

Dot-to-dot activities help to practise the order of numbers from 1–10. Encourage your child to identify the colours red, blue, yellow, and pink in their environment. To help your child read the word of the colour, make a label and attach it to an object of that colour.

Answers:
8–9 Fun and games
10–11 Getting dressed

8

What comes next? Continue the pattern.

Draw and colour the same picture.

9

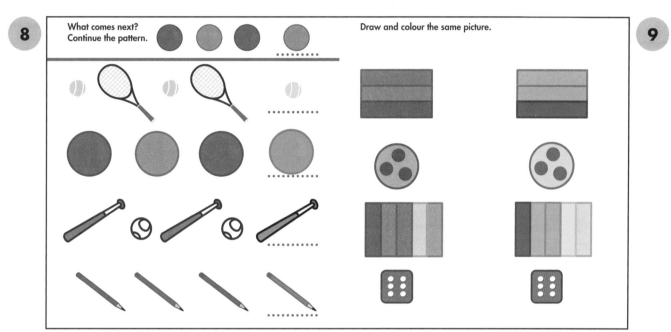

Recognizing and creating patterns is both fun and an important aspect of a child's development. Make your own patterns using buttons, beads, or even small toys and then encourage your child to copy and then make their own. Talk about things that match and are the same. This will help develop their skills of observation.

10

In each row, circle the odd one out.

Draw lines to match the shoes.

11

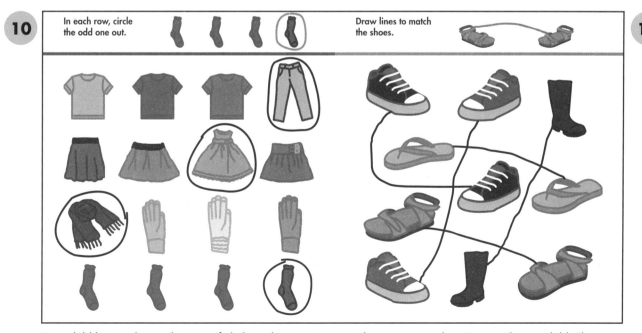

Your child has to choose the item of clothing that is not the same. This helps them to focus on looking at ways things can be different by shape or by colour. Play matching games such as Snap with your child. These observation skills are helpful not only in maths but also in early reading to differentiate the shapes of letters.

Answers:

12-13 Feeding time
14-15 Plant shapes

12 Draw a line from the animal to its food.

13 The zoo-keeper has some fish for the penguins. Show the path he takes to get to them.

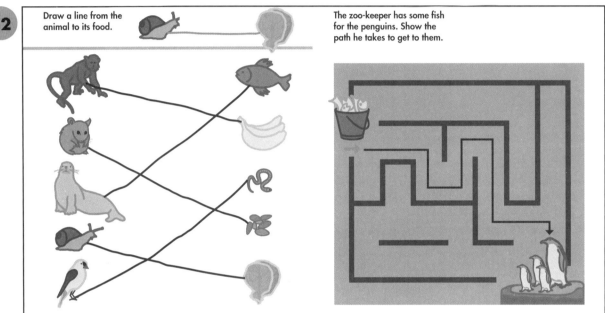

Making connections and putting things into categories helps to make sorting meaningful and useful in everyday life. Mazes are a fun way to encourage your child to grasp both the idea of direction and the awareness of space. Talk with your child as she/he moves her/his finger around the maze, using terms such as forwards, sideways, and downwards.

14 Circle the odd one out.

15 Match the leaves that are the same shape.

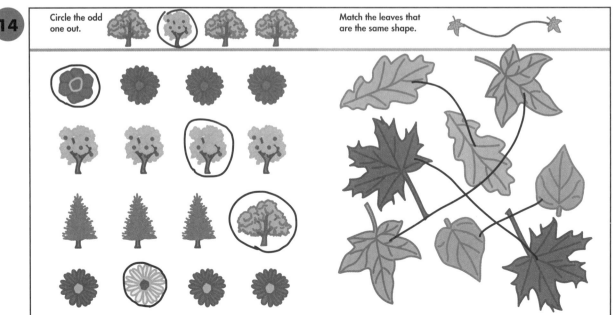

Discuss with your child the differences she/he can spot on this page, such as different shapes, colours, and numbers of things. Encourage your child to notice the small differences when looking at the collection of leaves: some may be pointed, others round, some rough, and others smooth.

Answers:

16–17 At the shops
18–19 In the bedroom

16 Tick (✔) the pictures that show something is inside.

17 Circle three things you would buy for a party.

Positional words and their meaning is an important part of your child's language. Talk with your child about the meaning of inside and outside and see if she/he can give other examples. Sorting things into categories is encouraged here with a practical example. Discuss what else may be bought for a party.

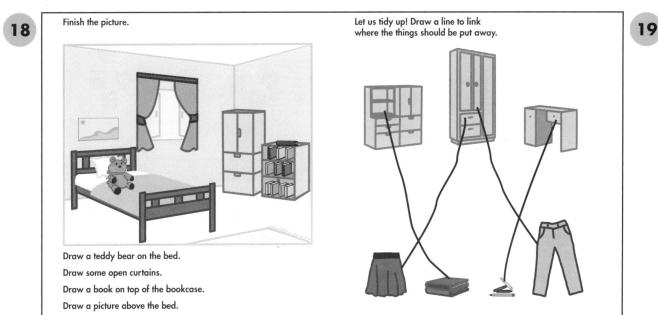

18 Finish the picture.

Draw a teddy bear on the bed.

Draw some open curtains.

Draw a book on top of the bookcase.

Draw a picture above the bed.

19 Let us tidy up! Draw a line to link where the things should be put away.

Here are some more positional words that are useful for your child to know: on, open, top, and above. Discuss with her/him the words that mean the opposite: off, closed, bottom, and below. Putting items into their right place develops skills of sorting, place, and position.

Answers:

22–23 Animal homes
24–55 Tree tops

22 Lead the animals to their homes. Follow the lines with a pencil.

23 Count the animals in their homes.

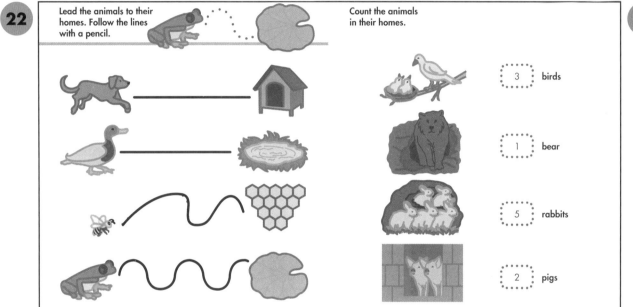

3 birds

1 bear

5 rabbits

2 pigs

This page develops pencil control, eye- and hand- coordination, and builds up concentration, which are all useful skills in Maths to write numbers, coordinate movement, and analyze data. Offer your child plenty of praise and encouragement as she/he works through the pages.

24 Circle the tallest.

Circle the widest.

Circle the smallest.

25 Draw the right number of apples on each tree.

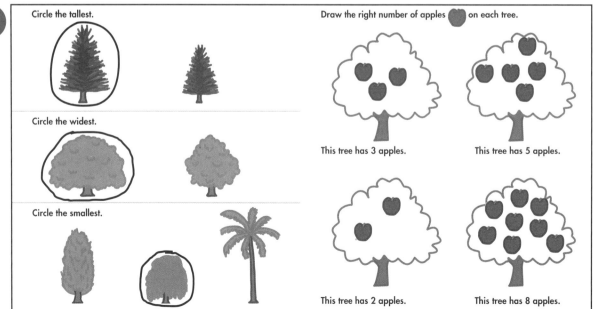

This tree has 3 apples.

This tree has 5 apples.

This tree has 2 apples.

This tree has 8 apples.

Here are some further words used to compare size. If your child is struggling to spot the difference, then talk about the activity first. If your child needs practical support for counting, then provide her/him with counters or a number line from 0 to 10.

Answers:

26–27 Jobs people do
28–29 In the kitchen

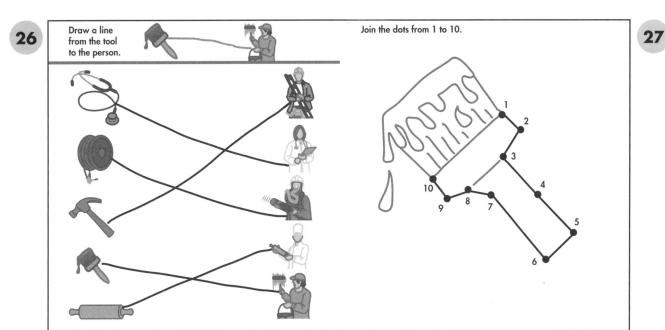

26 Draw a line from the tool to the person.

Join the dots from 1 to 10. **27**

Before beginning this page, talk about the jobs people do and the sort of tools and equipment they need. Check that your child can recognise the jobs shown: builder, doctor, fire fighter, baker, and painter. Later, your child's matching and sorting skills will be used to put numbers and items into sets.

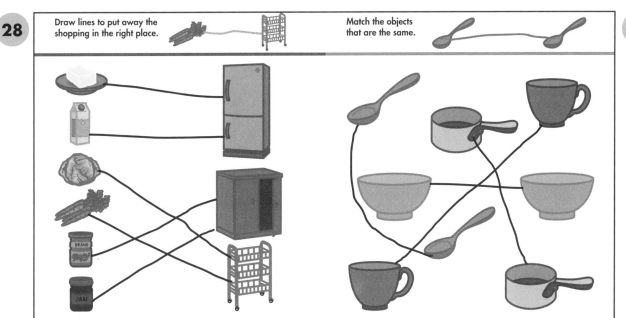

28 Draw lines to put away the shopping in the right place.

Match the objects that are the same. **29**

These activities continue to develop sorting and matching skills. The time filler challenge encourages your child to think of positions of things in relation to each other. Is the sink to the left, right, or in front of a table? As you help your child draw the plan, encourage her/him to use positional words.

Answers:

30–31 Animal moves
32–33 Pick and mix

30 Continue the lines to show how the animal moves.

31 Draw the legs onto each body to match.

Talk with your child about the shapes that the movement of animals make, using shape language such as curve, straight, and round. The number of animal legs is a fun example of counting as well as making some useful observations about the differences between animals.

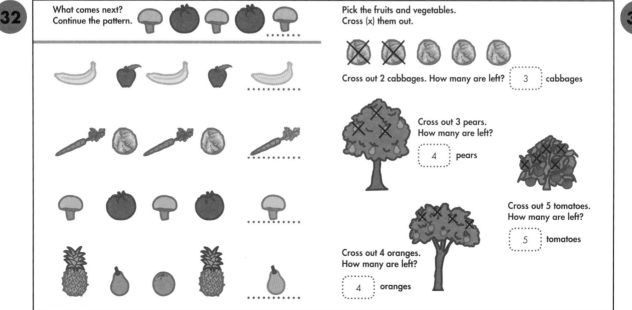

32 What comes next? Continue the pattern.

33 Pick the fruits and vegetables. Cross (x) them out.

Cross out 2 cabbages. How many are left? 3 cabbages

Cross out 3 pears. How many are left? 4 pears

Cross out 5 tomatoes. How many are left? 5 tomatoes

Cross out 4 oranges. How many are left? 4 oranges

Encourage your child to think not only about what comes next in the pattern but also what comes after that. Can they keep going with the sequence of three at the bottom of the page? The activity on page 33 introduces the idea of subtraction or counting back. Discuss with your child how many items there are to begin with before crossing out.

Answers:
34-35 On the move
36-37 Meal times

34

Colour the vehicles.

35

The lorry is making a delivery to the shop. Show the way to get there.

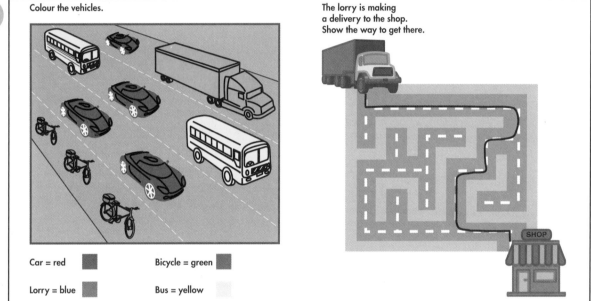

Car = red

Bicycle = green

Lorry = blue

Bus = yellow

SHOP

Help your child connect the vehicle name with the picture. Once they have completed the colouring activity, encourage them to count how many of each vehicle there are. For the time filler challenge, take a piece of paper with you and show your child how they can make a mark each time they see a vehicle. Introduce the idea of a tally for every five marks.

36

Circle the things you would have for breakfast.

37

Pick the food and drinks. Cross (x) them out.

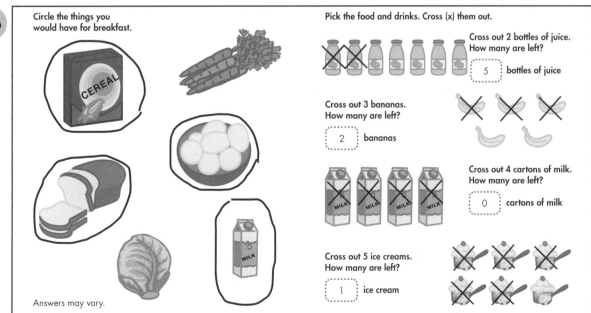

CEREAL

Cross out 2 bottles of juice. How many are left?

5 bottles of juice

Cross out 3 bananas. How many are left?

2 bananas

MILK

Cross out 4 cartons of milk. How many are left?

0 cartons of milk

Cross out 5 ice creams. How many are left?

1 ice cream

Answers may vary.

Meal times are wonderful opportunities for using maths in a practical way. Counting food items, talking about shapes and colours, taking measurements, and comparing sizes of amounts are some of the topics you can talk about. You can introduce the concept of sharing equal amounts when cutting a cake or a pizza.

Answers:

38–39 Animal patterns
40–41 Seed shapes

38

Circle the odd one out.

Draw the other half of this butterfly to match.

39

Discuss with your child what the similarities and differences are between the animals. For example, zebras and giraffes both have four legs and a tail, but are different in size, colour, and pattern. Matching the butterfly pattern can be tricky. If your child needs help, put a small mirror along the line of the butterfly's body so that she/he can see the pattern reflected.

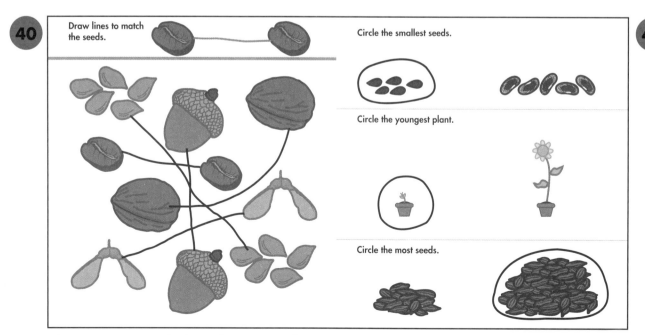

40

Draw lines to match the seeds.

Circle the smallest seeds.

Circle the youngest plant.

Circle the most seeds.

41

Objects in nature provide plenty of opportunities for maths investigations. These activities encourage your child to consider shape, size, and amount of things. You could discuss with your child how things such as a plant, an animal, or themselves change as they grow. Use language such as bigger/smaller, wider/narrower, and more/less.

Answers:

42-43 In the park
44-45 Toys and games

42 Connect the dots from 1 to 10.

43 Colour the picture.

1 = red   2 = green   3 = yellow   4 = blue

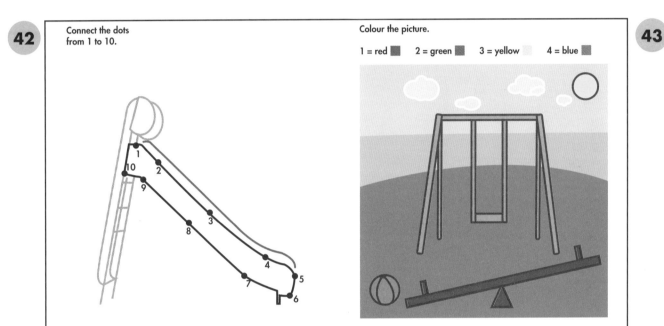

These activities offer more opportunities for counting up and recognizing numbers. The park is another great place where number and other maths terms can be used. How many people are on the climbing frame? What colour is the swing? What shape is the roundabout? How many steps are there on the ladder?

44 Some of these toys have wheels and others do not. Draw lines to put the toys in the correct set.

No wheels

Has wheels   No wheels

45 Draw the same picture.

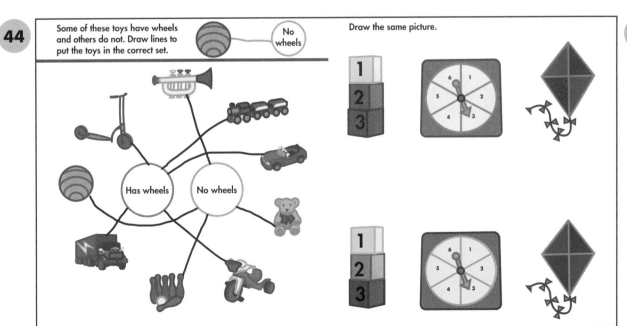

The word "set" is used instead of "groups" as it is a word that your child will also need to know for school. Can they think of any other toys that belong in these sets? Talk about the shapes your child will need to draw to copy the pictures: some have straight lines and others have curved lines.

Answers:

48–49 Animal patterns
50–51 Seed shapes

48 · **49**

Draw the other half of the lion.

Draw two wide eyes on the owl.

Draw a long trunk on the elephant.

Draw some large ears on the rabbit.

Draw some sharp teeth on the crocodile.

These activities continue to expand your child's maths language, which will be used when comparing shapes and sizes of things. Together, look in a mirror and talk about what is the same and what is different on either side of your faces. Do your hairstyles make the two sides different or are there other features too, such as freckles?

50 · **51**

Circle the odd one out.

Tick (✔) the three things a plant needs to grow.

Following instructions is another useful skill for developing a range of maths skills and thinking about doing things in the right order. To extend the growing sunflower activity, help your child to record what days of the week she/he water her/his plants and measure how tall they are once a week.

Answers:

52–53 Sports
54–55 At home

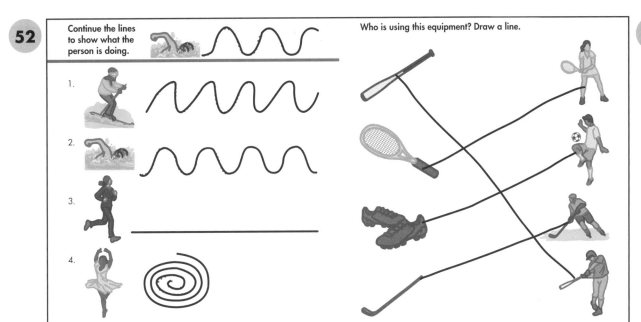

52 Continue the lines to show what the person is doing.

1.
2.
3.
4.

53 Who is using this equipment? Draw a line.

These pages encourage your child to look at patterns, think about shapes, and make connections. Watch some sport either live or on television with your child and talk about the number of players, the shapes and sizes of the pitch, balls, and other equipment, and adding on the scores.

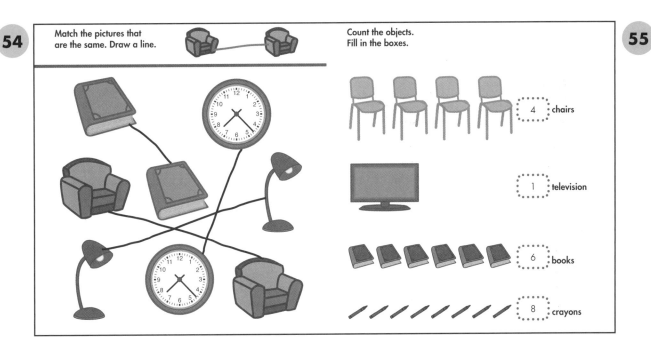

54 Match the pictures that are the same. Draw a line.

55 Count the objects. Fill in the boxes.

4 chairs

1 television

6 books

8 crayons

Check that your child is writing the numbers correctly, starting from the top. It is important that they begin to learn how to write the numbers correctly as it is very difficult to unlearn mistakes. Your house is a great place to find and count things. You can extend the time filler by setting further 10-minute challenges of finding a certain number of things beginning with a particular letter.

Answers:

56–57 Animal sizes
58–59 Seasons

56 Circle the biggest.

Circle the tallest.

Circle the heaviest.

57 Put these animals in size order 1st, 2nd, and 3rd. Start with the smallest. Write your answers in the ribbons.

Talk about the opposites of these size-related words to build your child's mathematical language. Look out for opportunities, such as in competitions or comparisons of sizes of things, to use the words 1st, 2nd, 3rd etc.

These will help your child learn these positional terms. Your child's picture of the zoo will provide a chance to discuss numbers and sizes of animals.

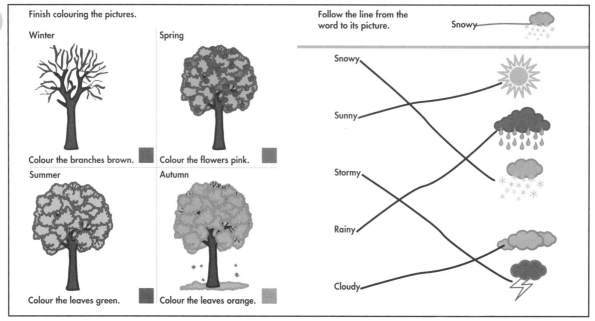

58 Finish colouring the pictures.

Winter — Colour the branches brown.

Spring — Colour the flowers pink.

Summer — Colour the leaves green.

Autumn — Colour the leaves orange.

59 Follow the line from the word to its picture.

Snowy
Sunny
Stormy
Rainy
Cloudy

Time is an important mathematical concept and your child is introduced to this by looking at the changing seasons. Show your child a calendar and talk about the days of the week and months of the year as well as the numbers. A further challenge would be to record the weather for a week by creating a chart and collecting data.

Answers:
60–61 At the beach
62–63 Bedtime

60

Circle the things you would take to the beach.

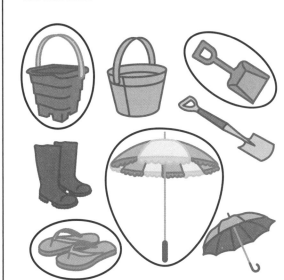

61

Finish the picture.
Draw a ball in front of the beach umbrella.
Draw a bucket behind the spade.
Draw the sun up in the sky.
Draw a towel on the sand.
Draw a flag on top of the sandcastle.

Wherever you go on holidays there will be opportunities to talk about numbers of things, spot shapes, and compare sizes. Position words

introducing "in front of" and "behind" are used again on this page.

62

What comes next?
Continue the pattern.

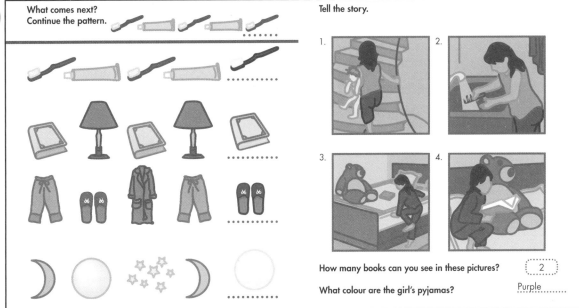

63

Tell the story.

1.
2.
3.
4.

How many books can you see in these pictures? `2`

What colour are the girl's pyjamas? Purple

The bedtime routine offers a chance to discuss the sequence of timings and the order of doing things.

Encourage your child to use the words first, second, third, and fourth when she/he is telling the story.

Answers:

20–21 All about me
46–47 All about me
64-65 All about me

My hobbies

Paste your picture here.

These pages encourage your child to talk about themselves and continue to make Maths relevant to their own lives. Their age and birthday use time-related words and counting skills are needed for numbers of family members and friends. Shapes, colours, and measurement skills are included in the questions. Ask your child further questions about the shapes they can see in their picture of the house. Use a measuring tape to measure other body parts or weigh your child on some scales. The time filler challenge encourages your child to design a poster all about themselves, which can lead onto asking more questions.

Me and my family